Crash!

Written by
ANN HARTH

Illustrated by
DION HAMILL

Steck Vaughn™

A Harcourt Achieve Imprint

www.Steck-Vaughn.com
1-800-531-5015

Crash!

Steck-Vaughn Take 3!
Originally published as Highlights! © 2005
Blake Publishing Pty Ltd, 108 Main Road,
Clayton South VIC 3168, Australia

Exclusive United States Distribution: Harcourt Achieve Inc.

Harcourt Achieve Inc.
10801 N. Mopac Exp., Bldg. 3
Austin, Texas 78759
www.HarcourtAchieve.com

ISBN-13: 978-1-4189-4490-2
ISBN-10:   1-4189-4490-4

Steck-Vaughn is a trademark of Harcourt Achieve Inc.

Printed in China

1 2 3 4 5 6 7 8 788 14 13 12 11 10 09 08 07

Contents

1. The Storm

Huddled in her seat on the airplane, Nalini thinks about home. When she said goodbye to her mother at the airport, she was excited about the trip to her cousin's small island. But now, with the plane in a storm, Nalini wants to be safe at home.

Nalini clutches her brother's hand and nervously peeks out the window, where black storm clouds loom and lightning flashes.

"Are you afraid?" Zed whispers. He keeps his voice steady so he'll sound brave, but Nalini feels his hand tremble.

Nalini looks seriously at her brother. "I'm terrified," she replies, glancing at the pilot, who is struggling to fly the plane. "Does the pilot know where we are?" she wonders.

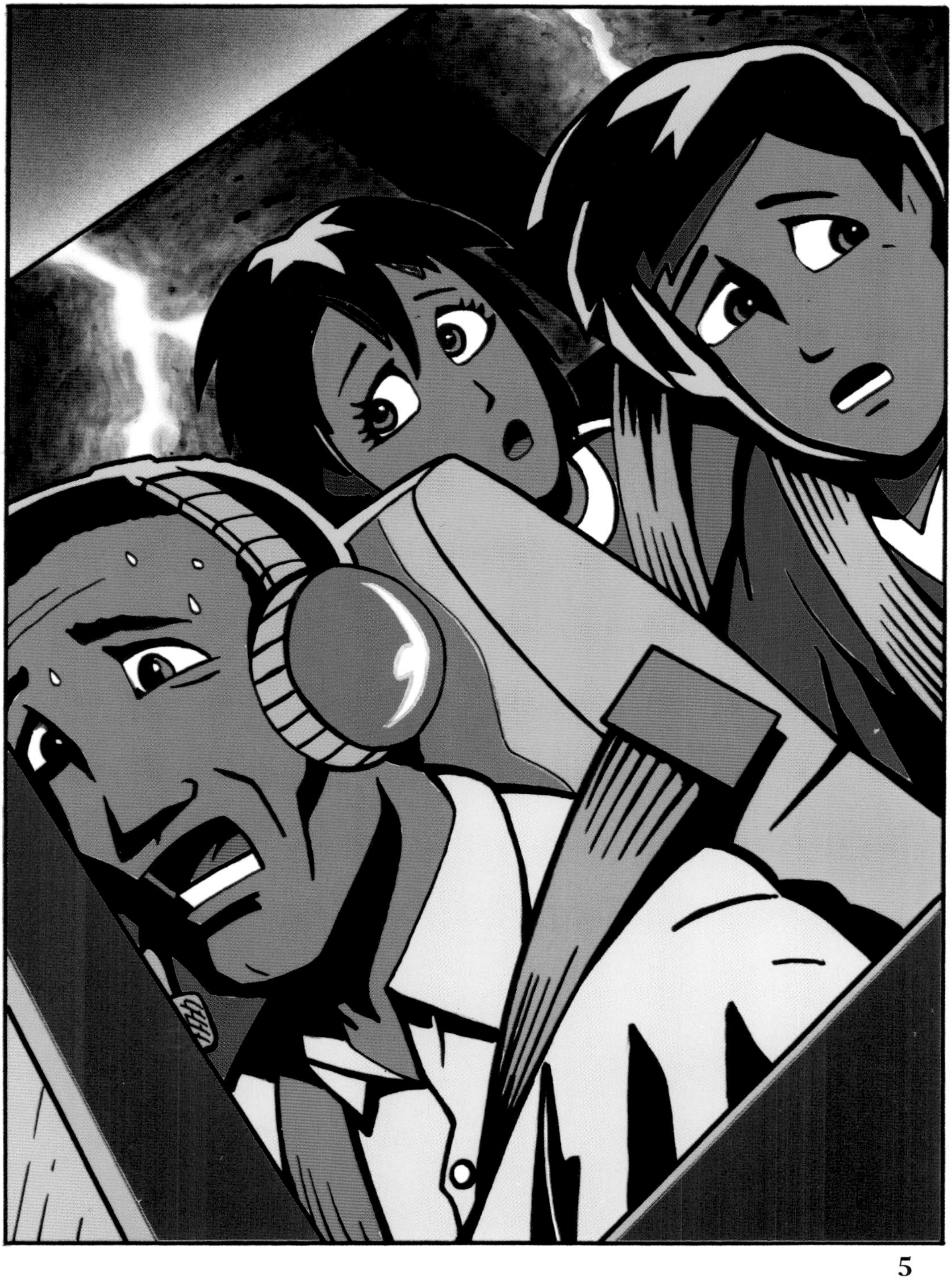

"Don't worry," Zed says, first tying Nalini's lifejacket and then tying his own. "I'll take care of you."

"I know," Nalini nods, but she doesn't believe Zed. "We're in a tiny airplane in a raging storm," Nalini thinks. "How can Zed take care of me?"

As lightning splits the sky and thunder booms, the pilot shouts into a microphone, pushes buttons, and shouts again. Yellow and red lights flash across the plane's instrument panel.

"Oh, no!" Zed yells.

Nalini looks through the window again, but this time, all she sees is the sea. She closes her eyes and braces herself. Someone screams, and then there is silence.

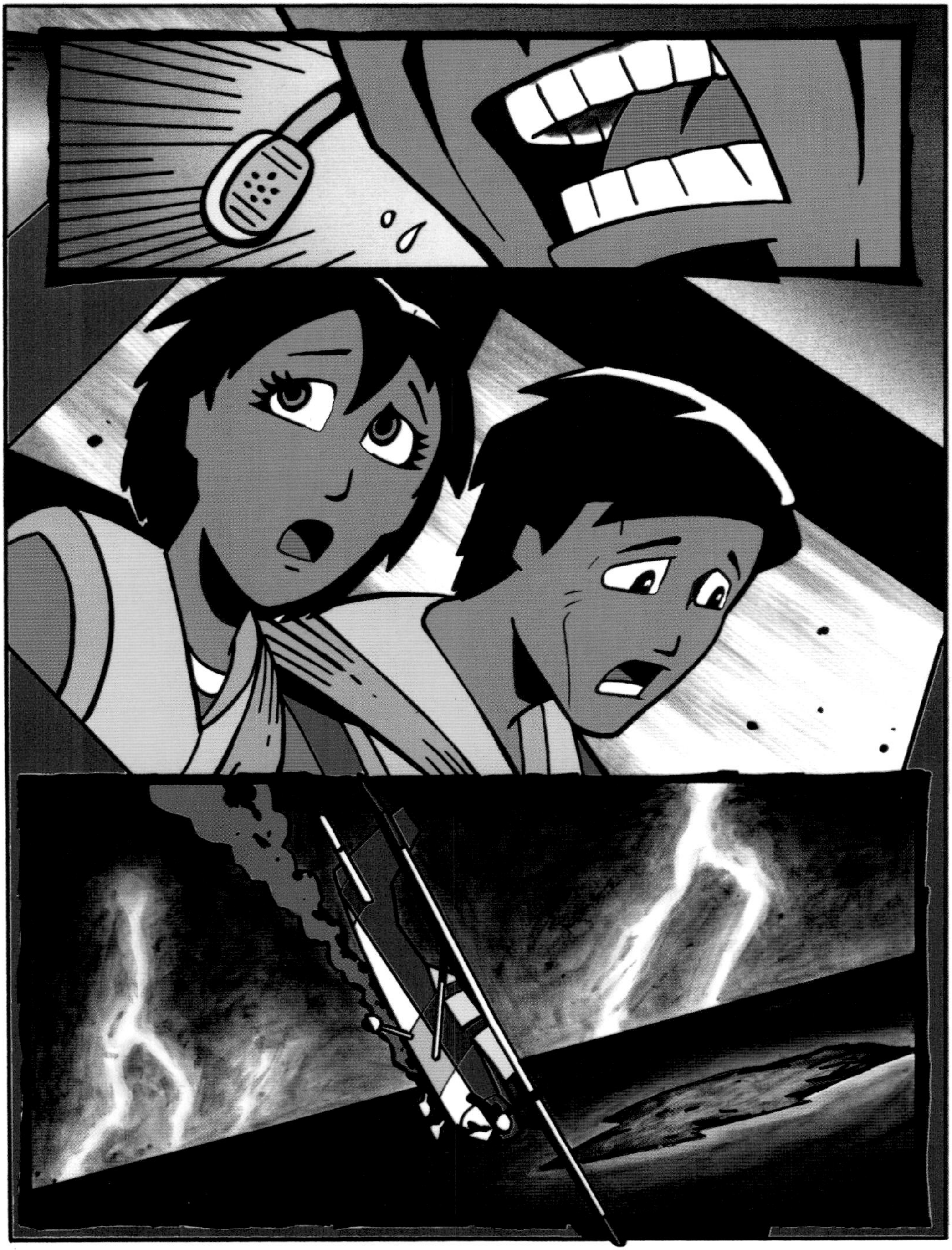

2. Alone

Nalini opens her eyes, blinking to clear the salt from her lashes. Her muscles ache and her clothes are drenched, but the storm is gone. She sits up slowly, dusting the gritty sand from her hair, skin, and clothes. A beach stretches out beside her and a rainforest rises up behind her.

She stands and looks around. "Zed, where are you?" she calls.

Pieces of the plane lie across the sand. Jagged, crumpled metal and plastic debris litter the beach. A backpack sits near the water.

Nalini removes her lifejacket and walks along the water's edge, calling Zed's name. When she reaches the rocks at the end of the beach, her throat is sore from shouting.

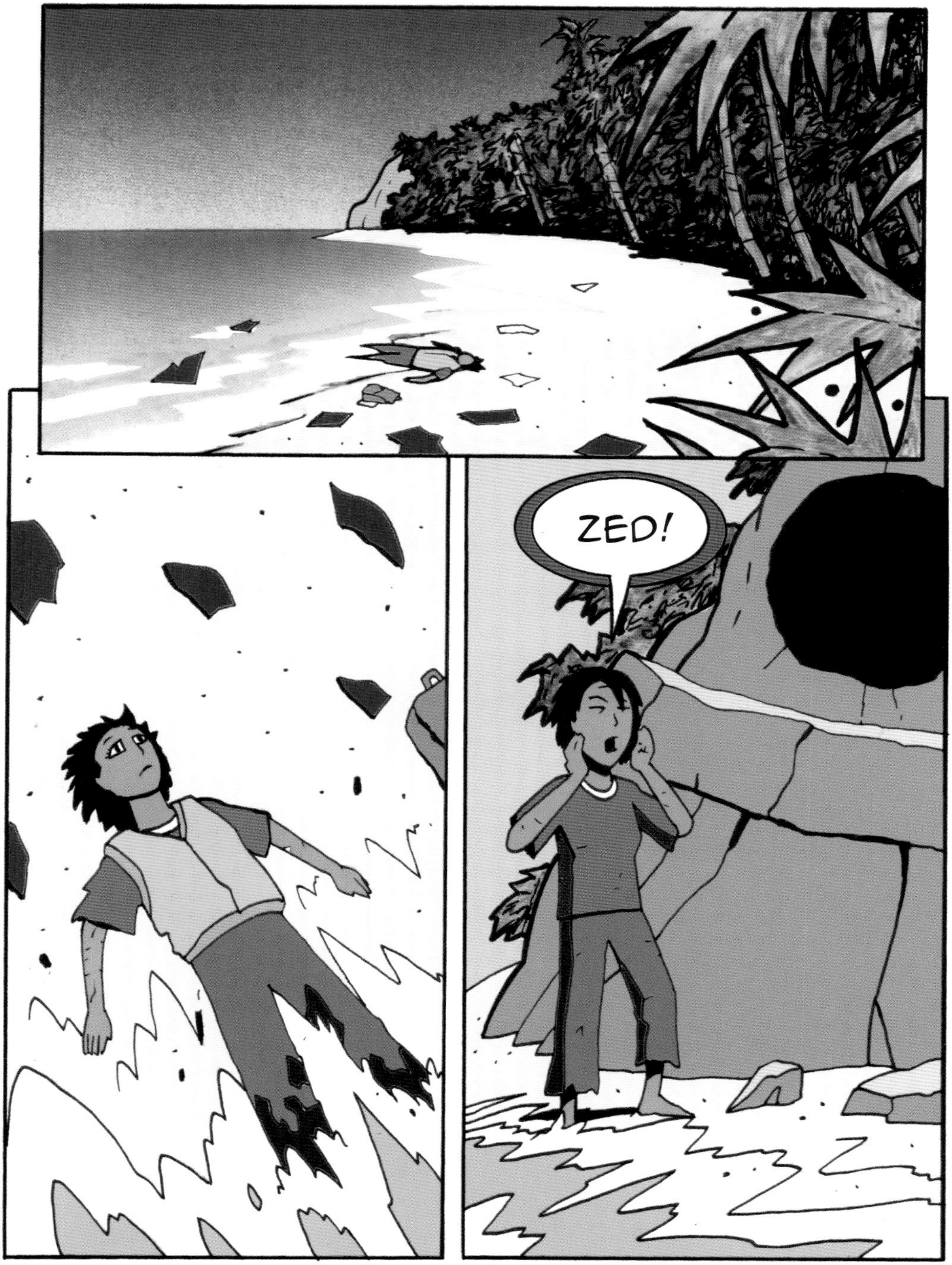
ZED!

Nalini climbs up the rocks to a ledge, where she sees a cave in the rock wall. She peers inside, but she can see nothing in the dark.

She faces the sea, continuing to call Zed's name, but no one answers. Zed and the pilot are nowhere to be found.

Nalini thinks about what her family would be doing now. Does her mother know Nalini and Zed are lost?

Nalini climbs back down to the beach. Walking slowly through the sand beneath the hot sun, she realizes how thirsty and exhausted she feels. Her lips are parched. She licks her lips to moisten them, but her tongue is dry. Nalini needs water.

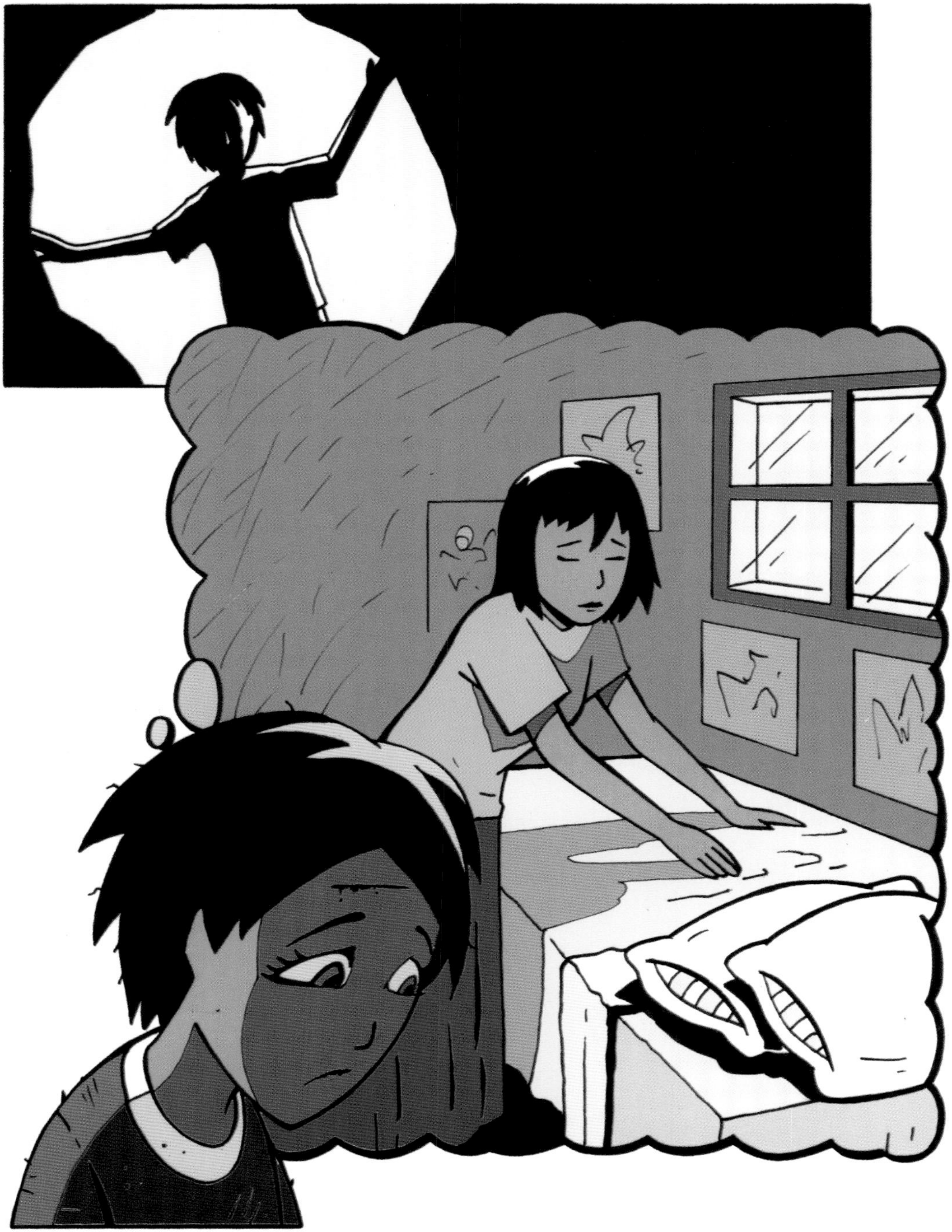

She looks at the sea. Water stretches as far as she can see, but it is too salty to drink.

Nalini walks a little farther, but stops when she sees a silver line running from the rainforest to the sea. "A stream!" she thinks. She sprints toward it, hoping it is not just her imagination.

She reaches the stream and tastes the water. "It is fresh! I can drink this water," Nalini says, sighing with relief. She follows the stream to a pool in the rainforest. She steps into the pool and gulps the cool water.

"I must find my brother," Nalini thinks. "Where are you, Zed? Are you alive?"

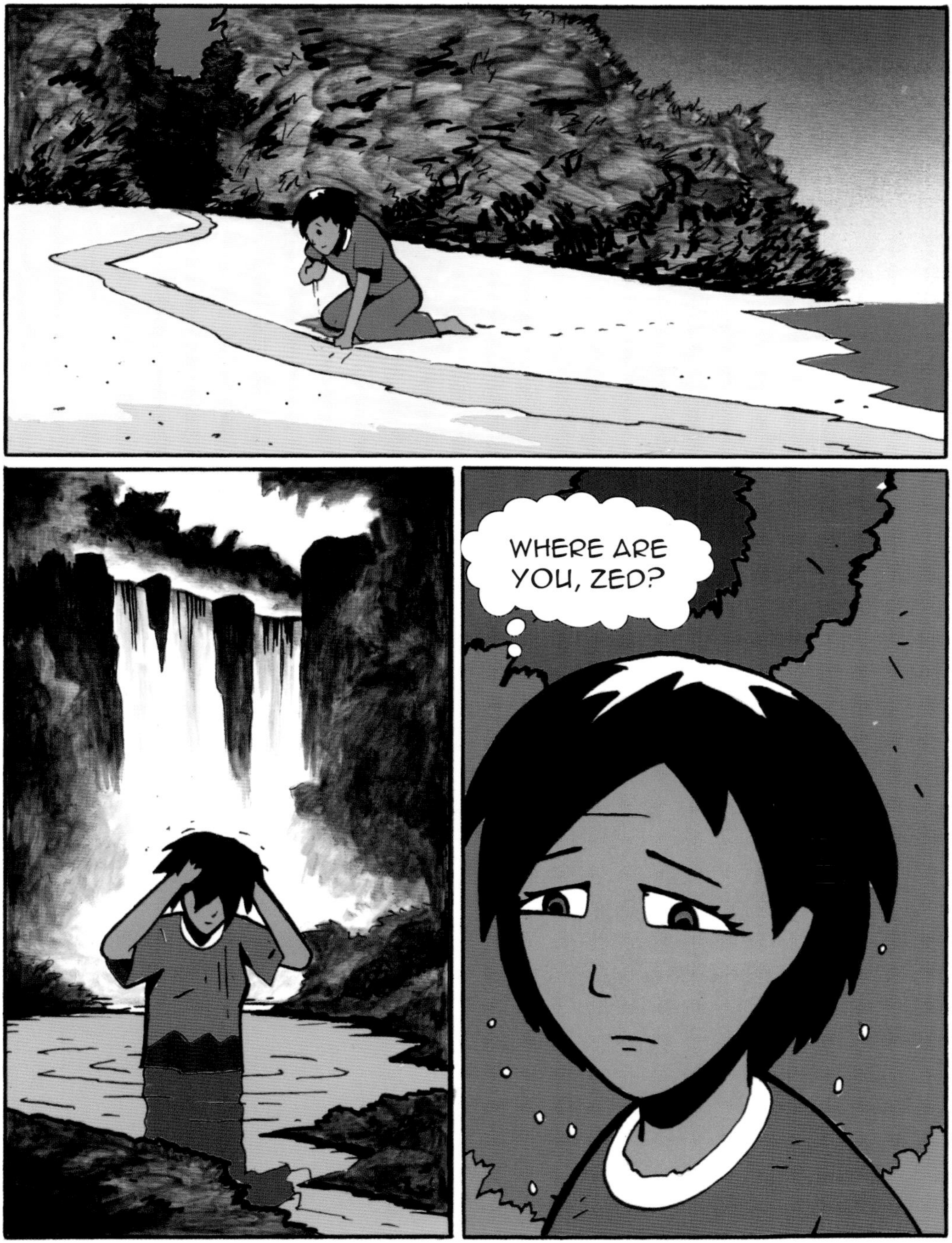
WHERE ARE YOU, ZED?

3. Zed Is Alive

Nalini scans the sea, carefully searching it for signs of human life, but she sees nothing . . . nothing . . . nothing. Suddenly she stops, then steps closer to the water.

Something is out there—something yellow, bobbing on the waves. Nalini plunges into the waist-deep water and begins to swim toward the object. As the waves carry it closer to the beach, Nalini swims faster. Soon she can see that it is a person in a yellow lifejacket.

"Zed!" she screams. With a surge of energy, Nalini reaches her brother, who is floating on his back with his eyes closed.

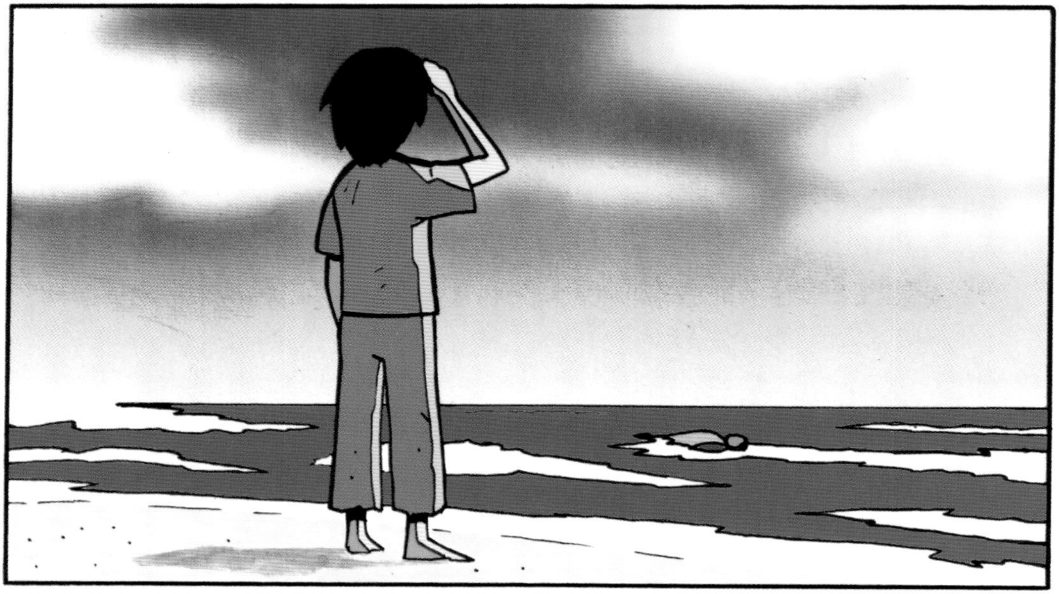

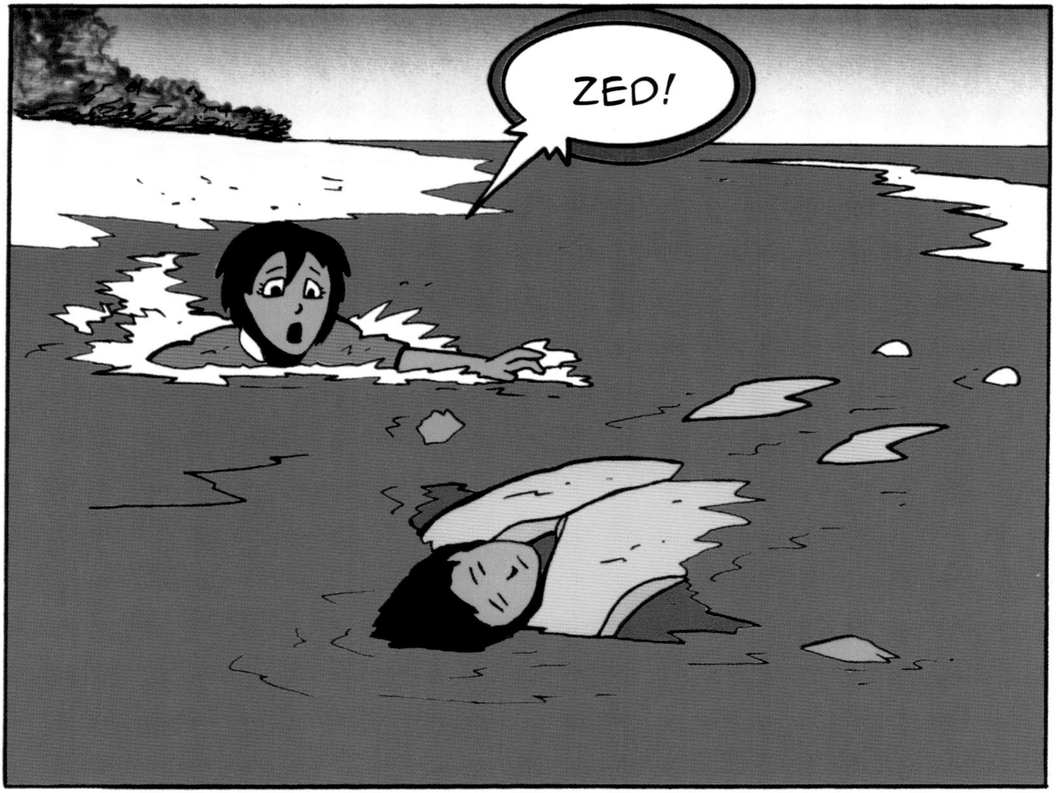
ZED!

Nalini swims in place beside him and gently touches his face. "Zed! Zed! Are you alive?" she shouts. She pushes fear and panic from her mind and concentrates on rescuing Zed. Grabbing the back of Zed's jacket, she swims to the beach. She hauls Zed onto the sand and kneels beside him. She places her trembling hand close to Zed's face and feels a tiny, warm puff of air.

"Oh, Zed, you're alive! Are you hurt? Do you need a drink?" Nalini asks, but Zed is too weak to answer.

"I'll take care of you," Nalini says, her voice shaking. "First, you need a drink."

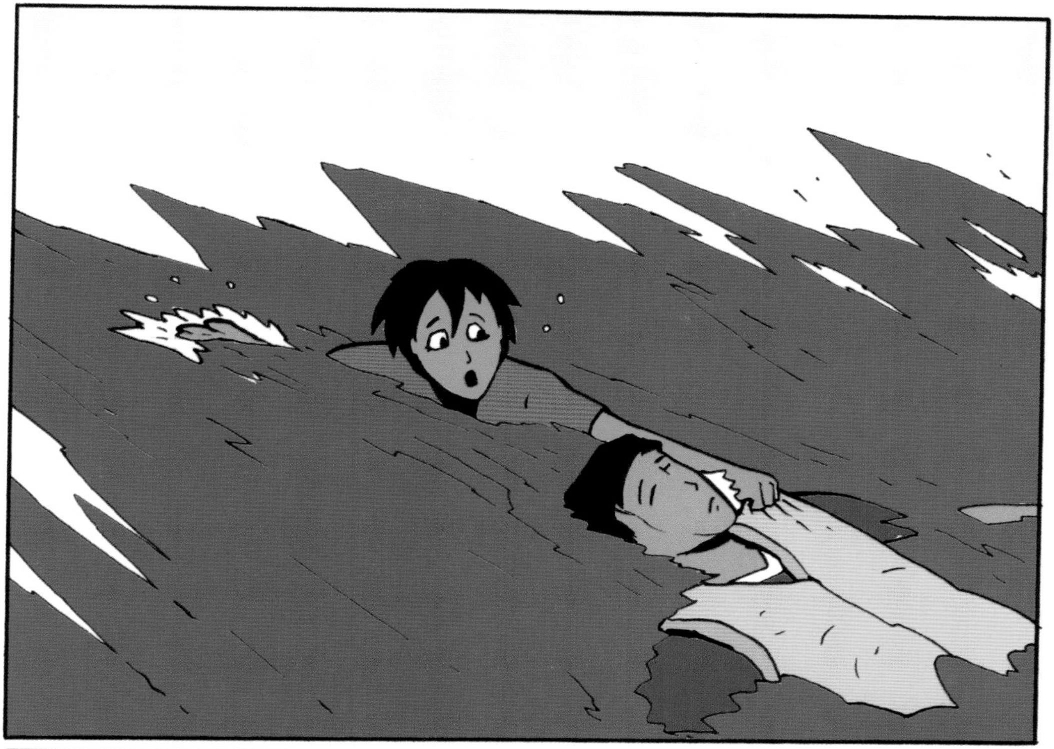

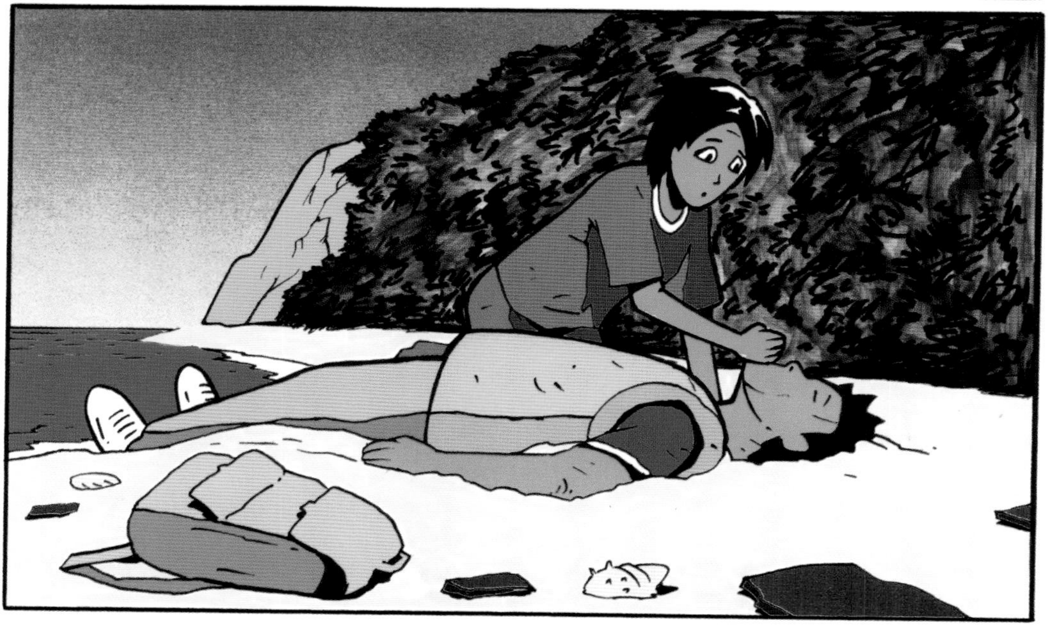

Nalini dashes to the backpack, looking for something to carry water. She empties the backpack onto the sand, rummaging through shirts, trousers, and socks. With sadness, she realizes that the clothes belong to the pilot. She wonders if he survived the crash, but she knows she has to take care of Zed now.

"I must get water quickly for Zed to drink, but how will I carry it?" Suddenly, she has an idea. She crams the clothes into the backpack and runs back to Zed.

"You need water, Zed. I know what to do! I'll be back."

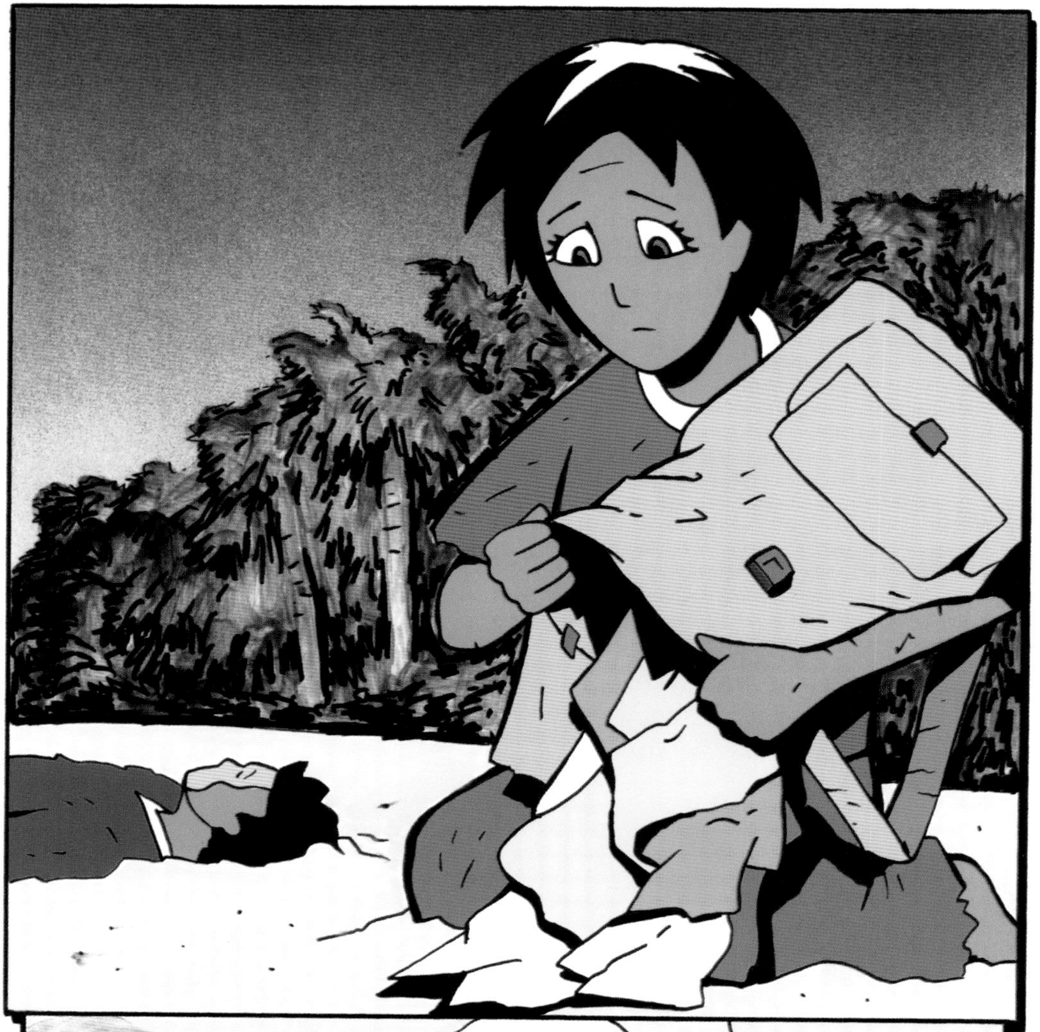

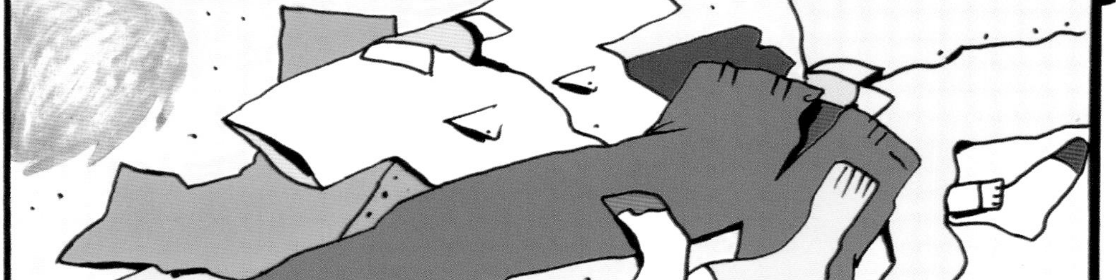

4. Zed's Drink

Carrying the backpack into the rainforest, Nalini hurries to the pool and drops the clothes into the water. She washes the saltwater away, places the drenched clothes in the backpack, and runs back to Zed.

"Here, Zed," Nalini says, squeezing a wet shirt over Zed's mouth. Zed swallows as Nalini continues to wring the water from the shirt. Relieved, Nalini smiles and squeezes the shirt until Zed stops drinking.

"Zed," Nalini says softly, "wake up. Another storm is coming."

Zed opens his eyes and looks at Nalini.

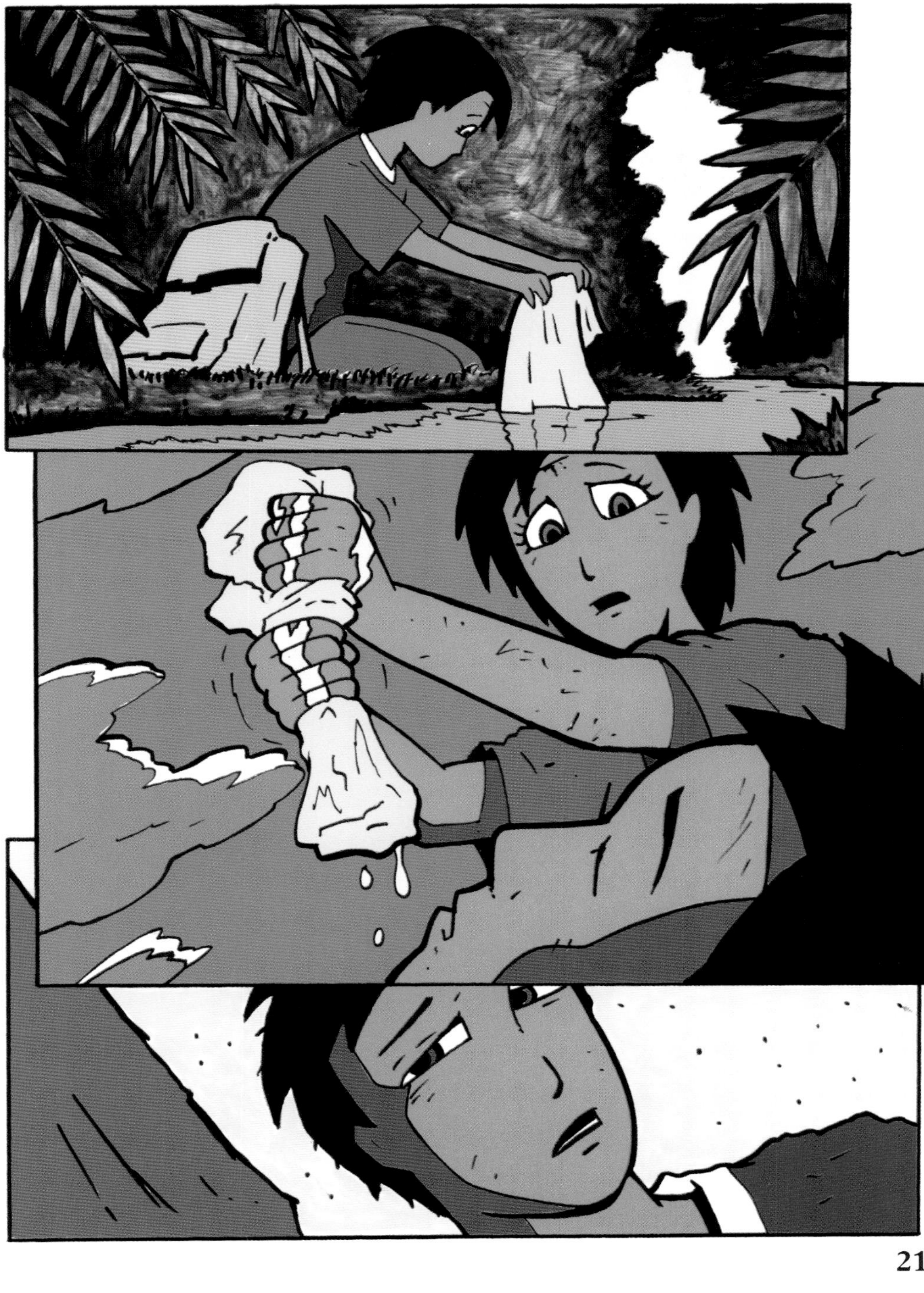

Strong gusts pick up dry sand on the beach as Nalini stares at the threatening black clouds drifting toward them. "We can't stay here, Zed. I found a cave that will protect us," Nalini says, gently touching Zed's arm.

"Ow!" Zed yells.

Nalini examines Zed's right arm. "Oh, Zed, I'm sorry. Your arm is swollen," Nalini says. "Can you move it?"

"No," Zed moans, wincing.

Nalini ties four socks together, making a sling to support his arm. "Is that better?" she asks, adjusting it over his shoulder and beneath his injured arm.

Zed nods. "A little," he replies.

"Can you walk?" Nalini asks. "We must hurry."

Zed stands up slowly. "I can walk," he mumbles. "I'll follow you."

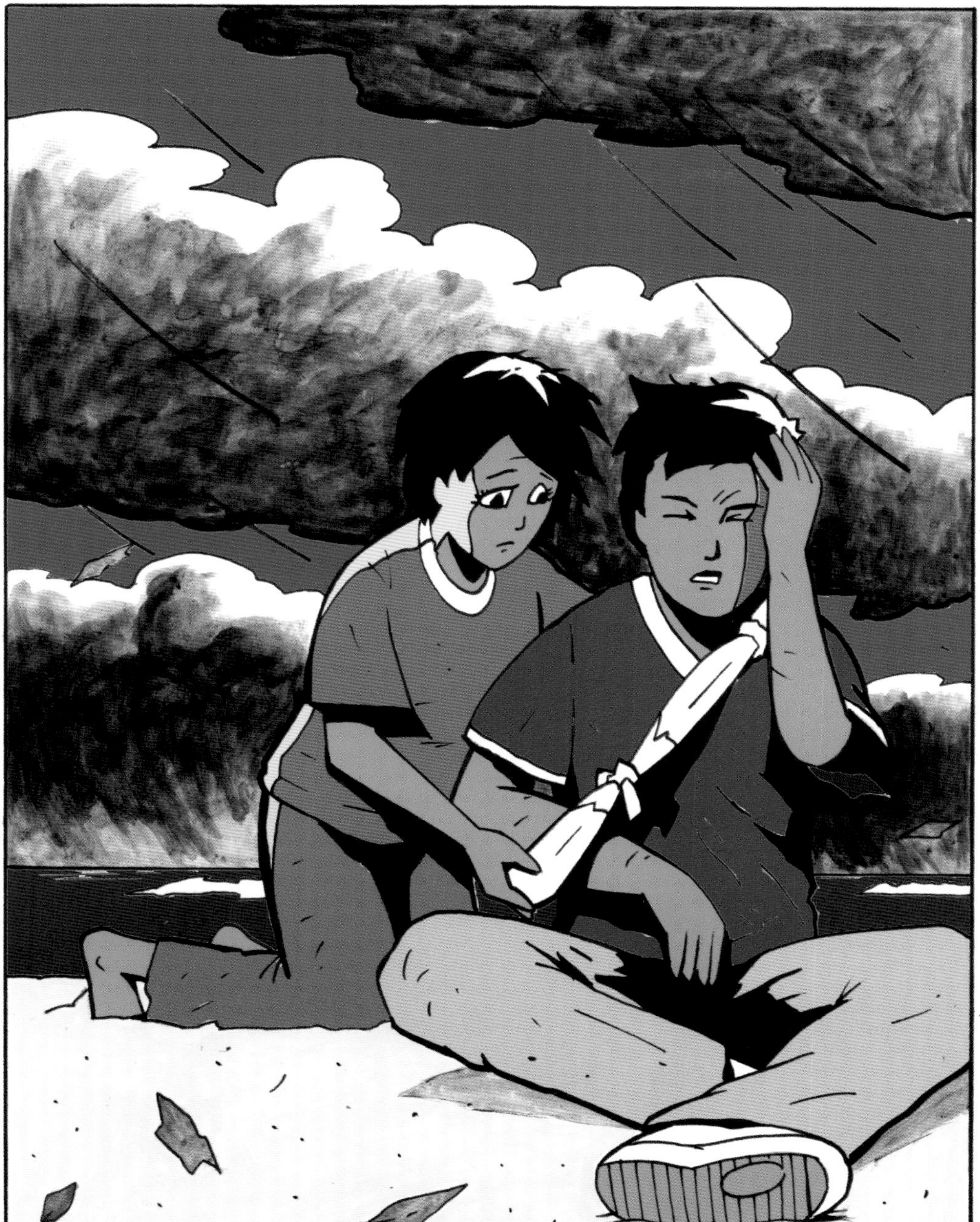

5. Another Storm

As Nalini and Zed walk toward the cave, they can see that the tide is coming in. The passage to the cave is narrower because of the water that is rising up the beach.

When they reach the rocks, Nalini climbs up and drops the backpack, then jumps back down to help Zed. "Ready to climb?" she asks.

"I think I am," Zed replies, but he struggles to climb with one arm. Nalini pushes Zed from behind. Finally, they reach the ledge, and Zed falls onto his back, exhausted.

As large raindrops begin to fall, Nalini looks into the dark cave. She wonders what's inside and if it's safe to enter. But then lightning hits the water as the storm approaches.

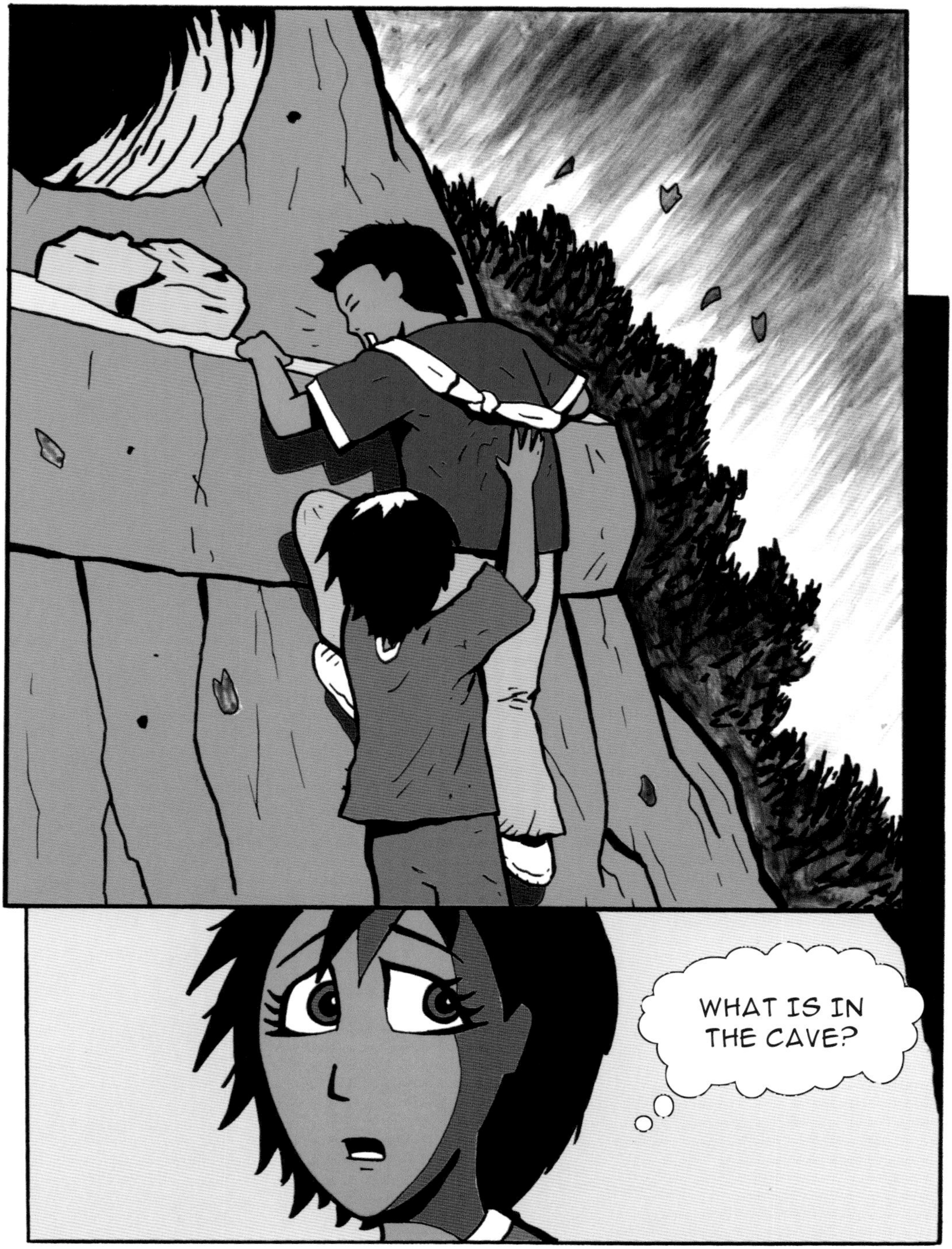
WHAT IS IN
THE CAVE?

"Come on, Zed," Nalini urges, helping him into the cave as the storm moves in.

Zed winces at the pain in his arm, and Nalini hears him stifle a moan. "What if Zed's arm is broken?" Nalini worries. She carefully helps Zed lower himself to the floor, where he stretches out and closes his eyes.

As the storm rages outside, Nalini sits close to Zed, listening as his breathing becomes even and deep.

Nalini is so tired she barely feels the hardness of the floor as she lies down next to Zed. "We are dry and safe for now, and tomorrow I will find us food," she says softly. Her eyes close, and she drifts off to sleep.

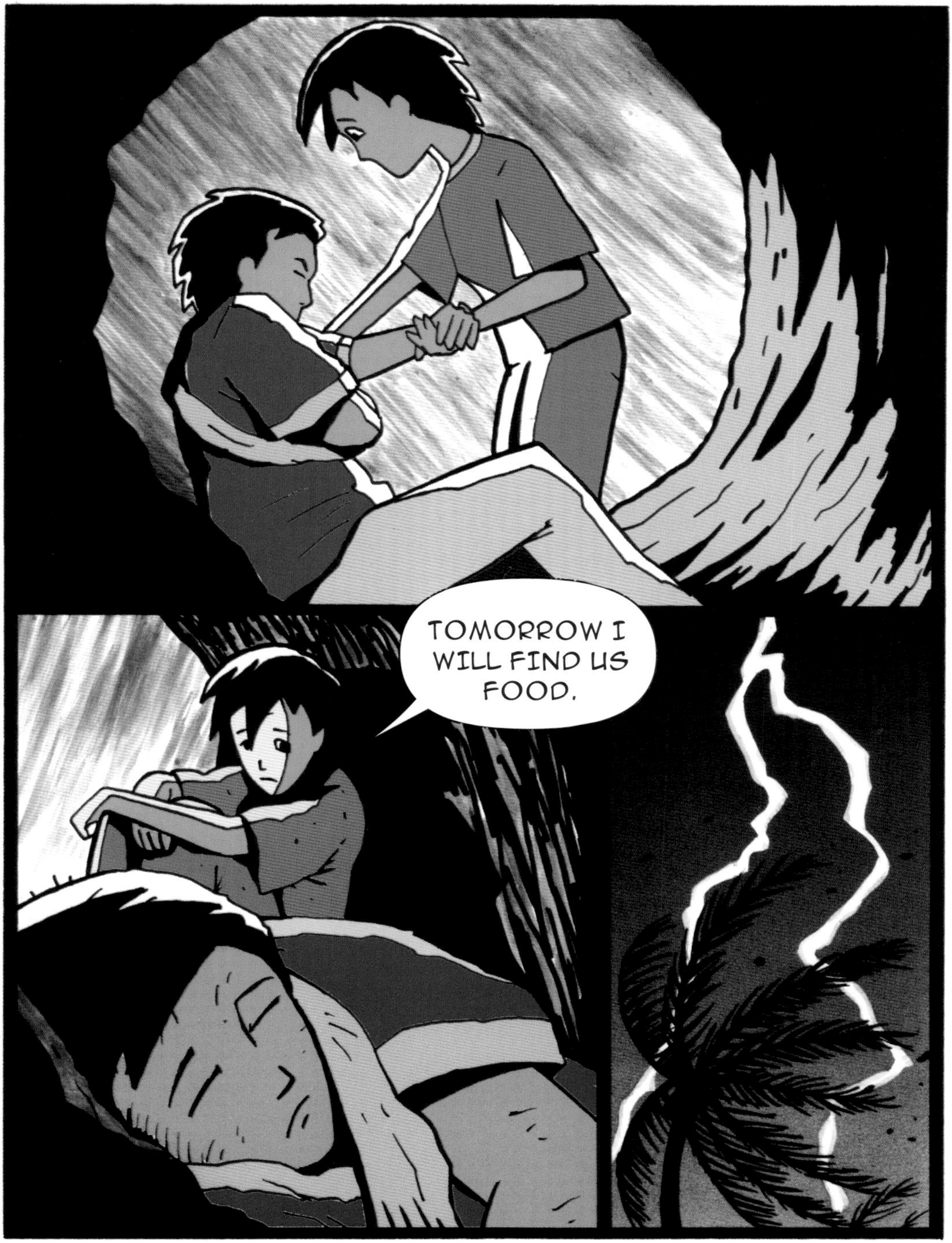
TOMORROW I WILL FIND US FOOD.

6. The Cave

When Nalini wakes up the next morning, sunlight illuminates the cave. Because of the light, Nalini is able to clearly see everything inside it for the first time. Except for a dark circle in the middle of the sandy floor, the cave is big and empty.

Nalini examines the dark circle and finds that it is a pile of burned wood and ash surrounded by stones. The circle is an old fire.

"Zed!" Nalini exclaims. "Someone else is here!"

"Nalini?" Zed asks sleepily, pushing himself up with his good arm.

"Look," Nalini says, "there's been a fire here!"

"So what?" Zed says irritably. "I'm hungry, and my arm hurts."

"I'm hungry too, Zed, but first I must get more water for us to drink."

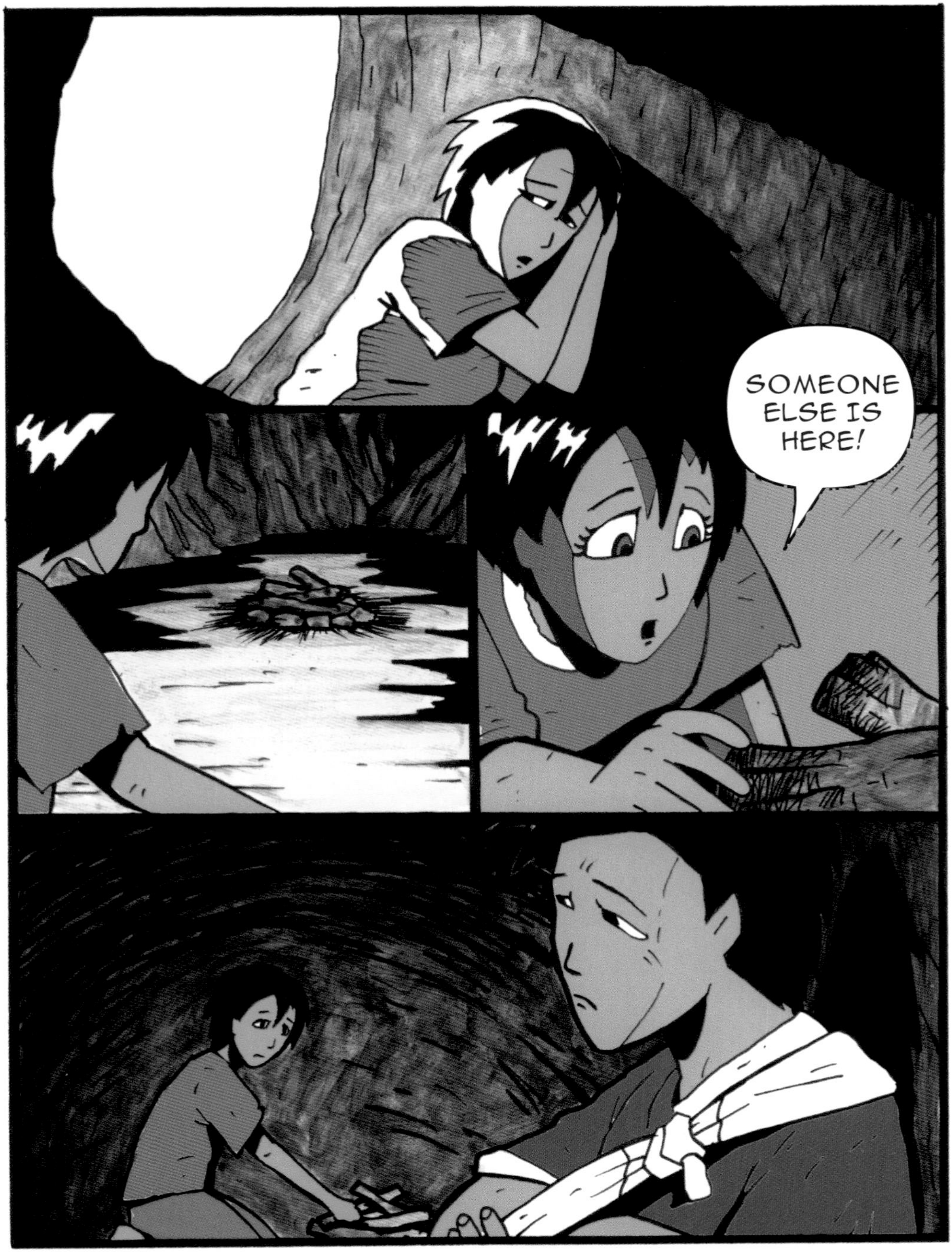
SOMEONE ELSE IS HERE!

"We should stay together. I'll come with you," Zed says. Nalini walks outside and scans the beach. She sees that the tide has risen closer to the rocks. "There's just enough time to get there and back if I hurry," Nalini thinks.

"I must hurry, Zed. Sit here in front of the cave. I'll come back soon," Nalini says, as she climbs down the rocks. "Don't worry. You can watch me all the way." But Zed still looks worried.

"I must bring water," Nalini says. "We need water to live."

"You're right," Zed agrees, "but please be careful. I'll watch you and listen for airplanes."

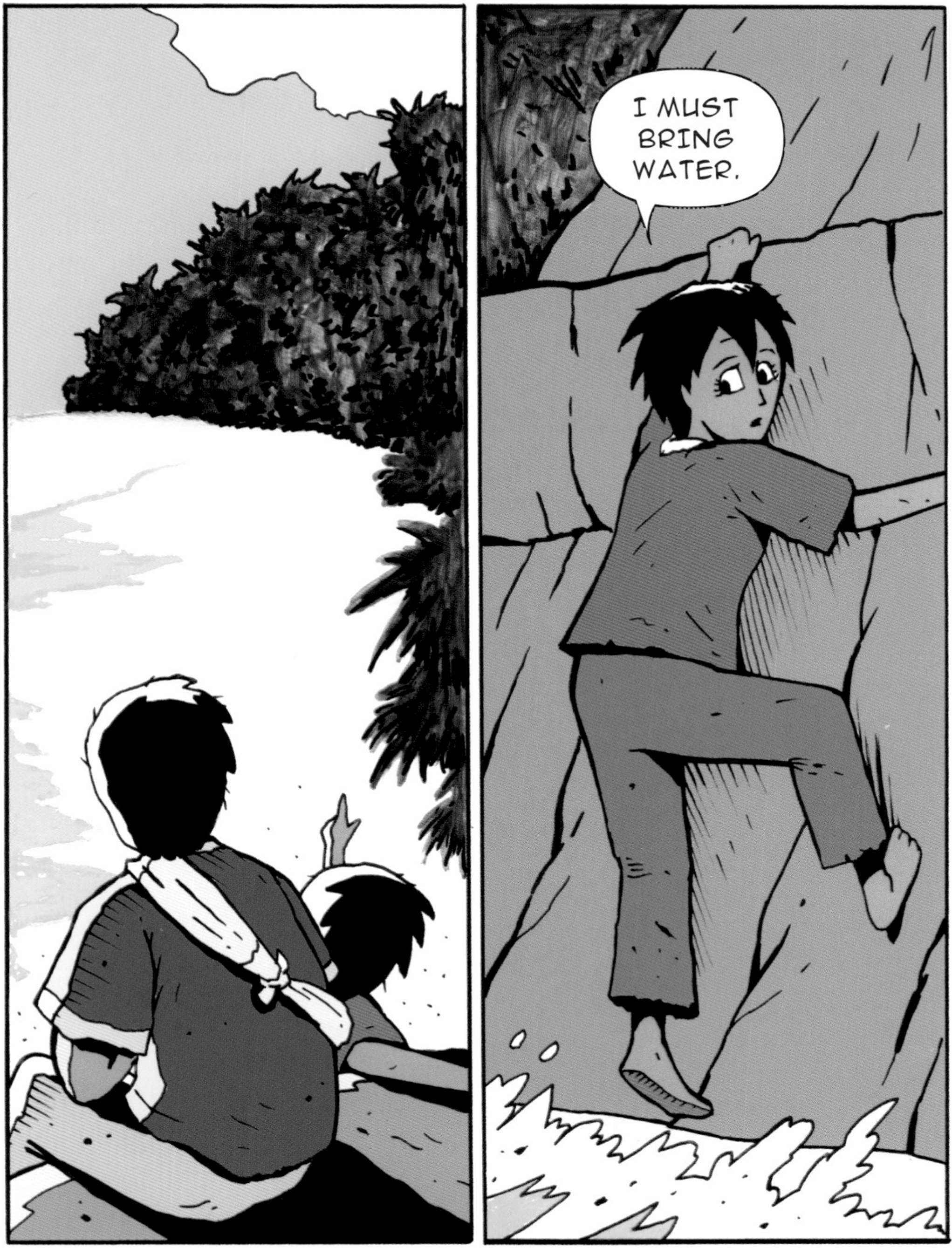
I MUST BRING WATER.

7. Water and Food

As Nalini hurries down the beach, she passes debris left by the storm. She reaches the stream and follows it into the rainforest. Examining seaweed caught in some tree roots, she spies something else and pulls the seaweed away.

"Three coconuts," Nalini says, delighted. When she picks one up and turns it over, water trickles out of a hole at one end. She notices that the other two coconuts have holes, too. "I can use these to carry water," Nalini thinks.

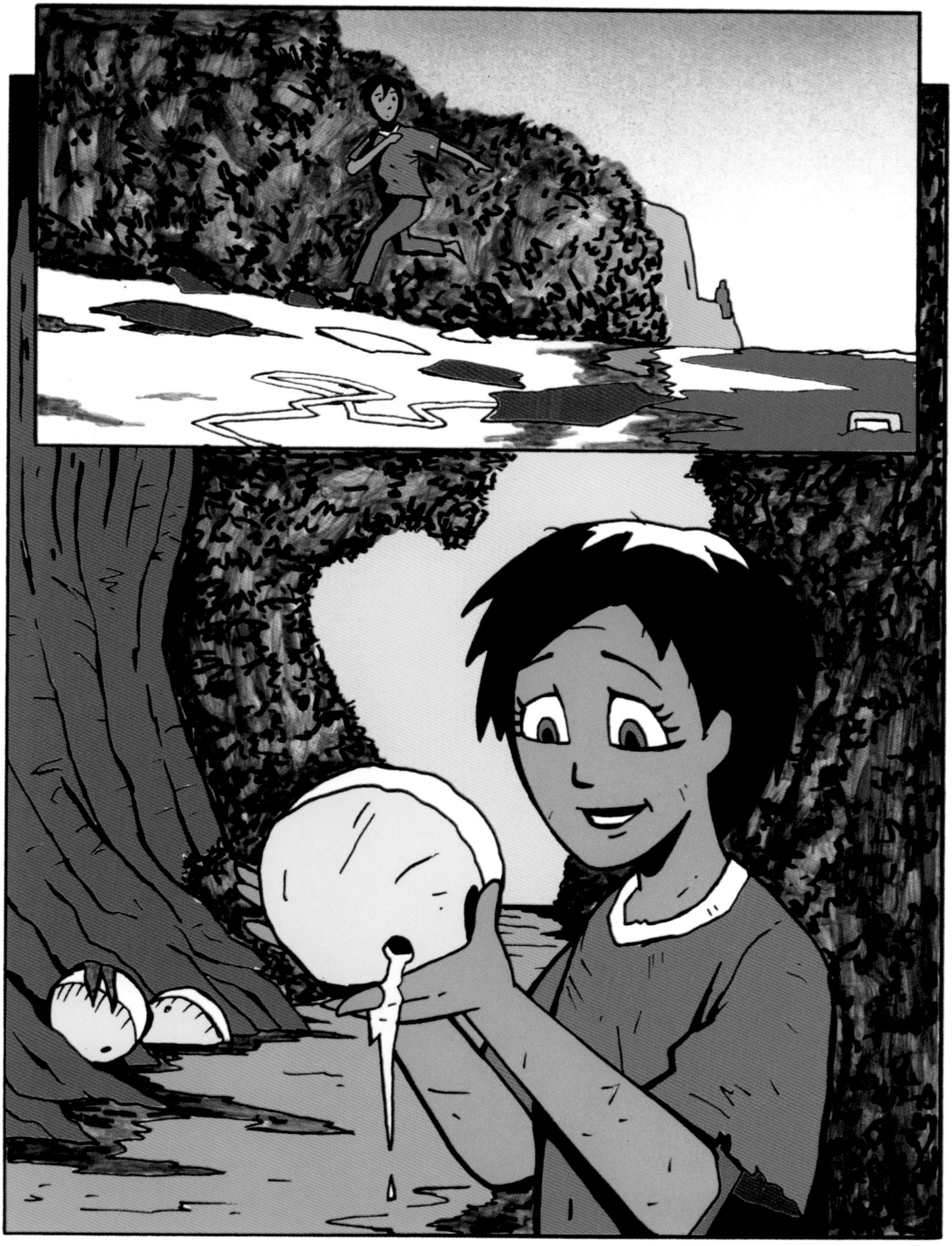

Nalini carries the coconuts to the pool, washes them, and fills them with fresh water. She sips the sweet-tasting water from one coconut. Balancing all three so they won't spill, she carries them toward the cave. "I must hurry," she thinks, as she crosses the sandy beach.

When she reaches the rocks, the seawater from the rising tide covers her ankles.

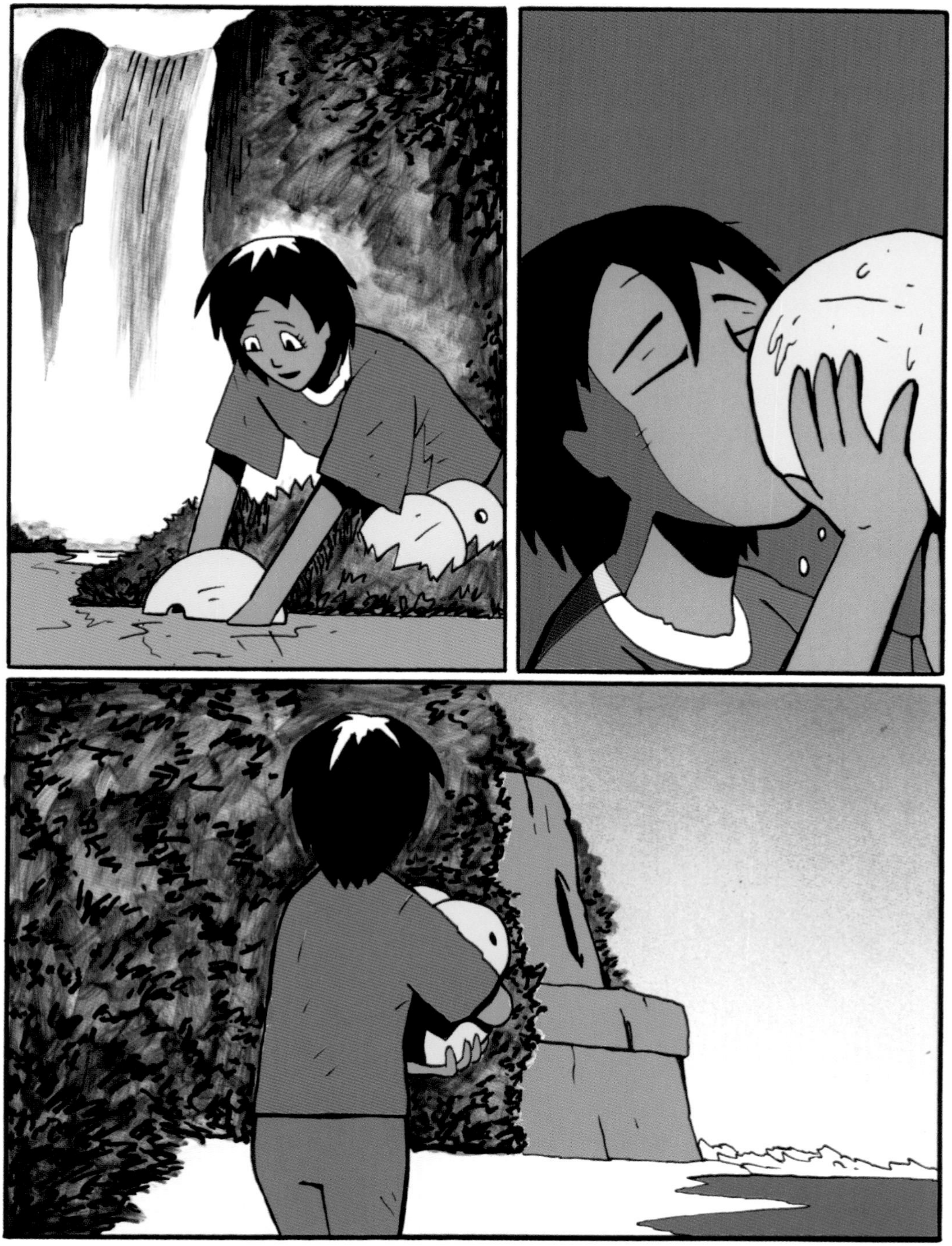

Nalini is about to climb up the rocks when she spots several coconuts beneath the palm trees. "We need food," she thinks.

"Nalini, please hurry!" Zed calls anxiously from the ledge.

"Here I am," Nalini calls back. "Throw down the backpack." Zed tosses it to her, and Nalini carefully loads it with the three coconuts full of water. She climbs to the ledge, and she and Zed drink water from one coconut, saving the other two for later. Then Nalini climbs down the rocks again.

"Where are you going?" Zed demands. "The tide is getting really high."

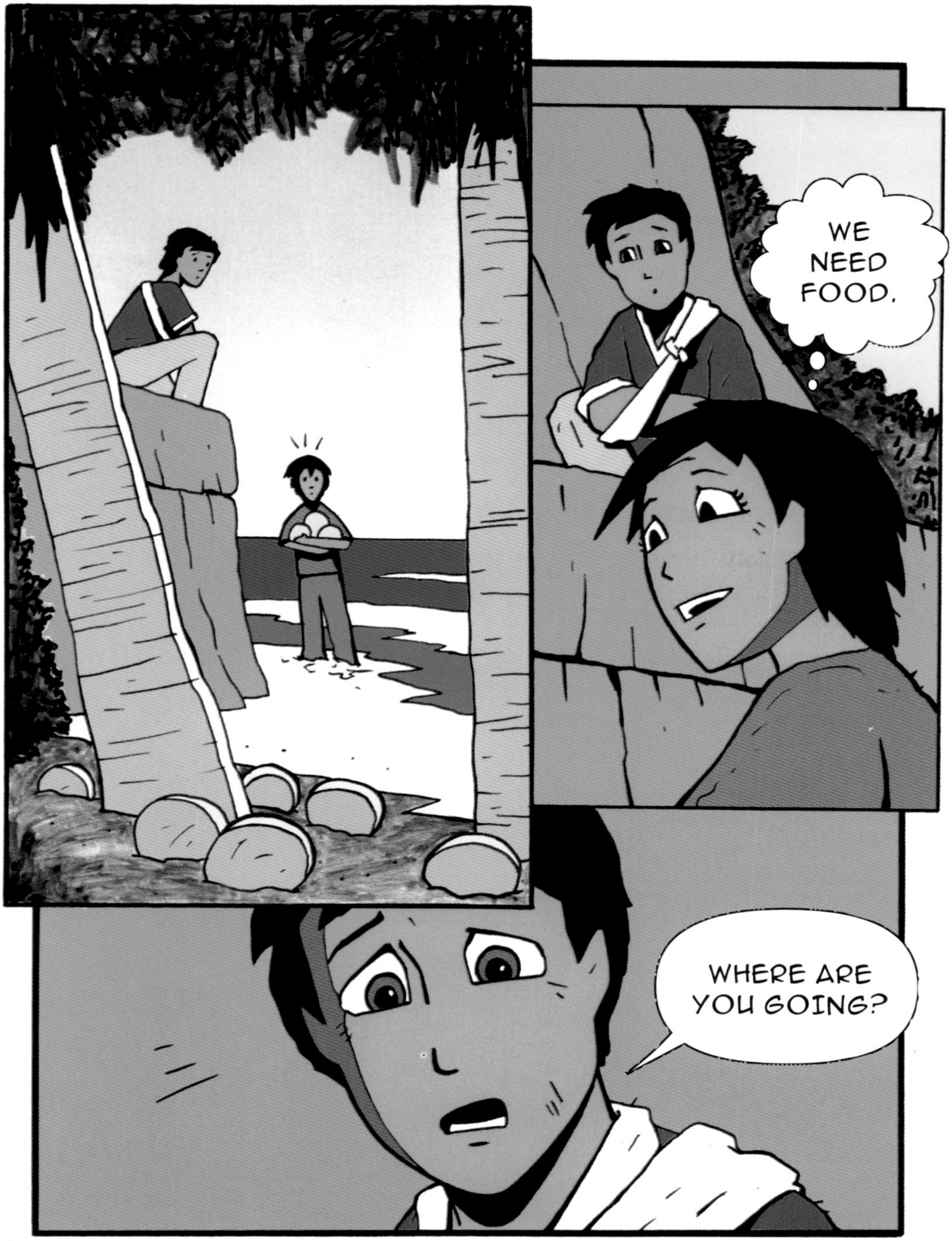
WE NEED FOOD.
WHERE ARE YOU GOING?

8. The Escape

"I'm not going far," Nalini calls, as she splashes to the edge of the water. She picks up a smooth, yellow coconut and tries unsuccessfully to open it. Suddenly, she sees two coconuts roll down the beach. Did they just fall from a tree?

She glances at the rising tide, wondering if she has time to grab the coconuts. She dashes toward them, picks them up, and notices both coconuts have cracks down the sides. "Food!" she exclaims, moving quickly toward the rocks.

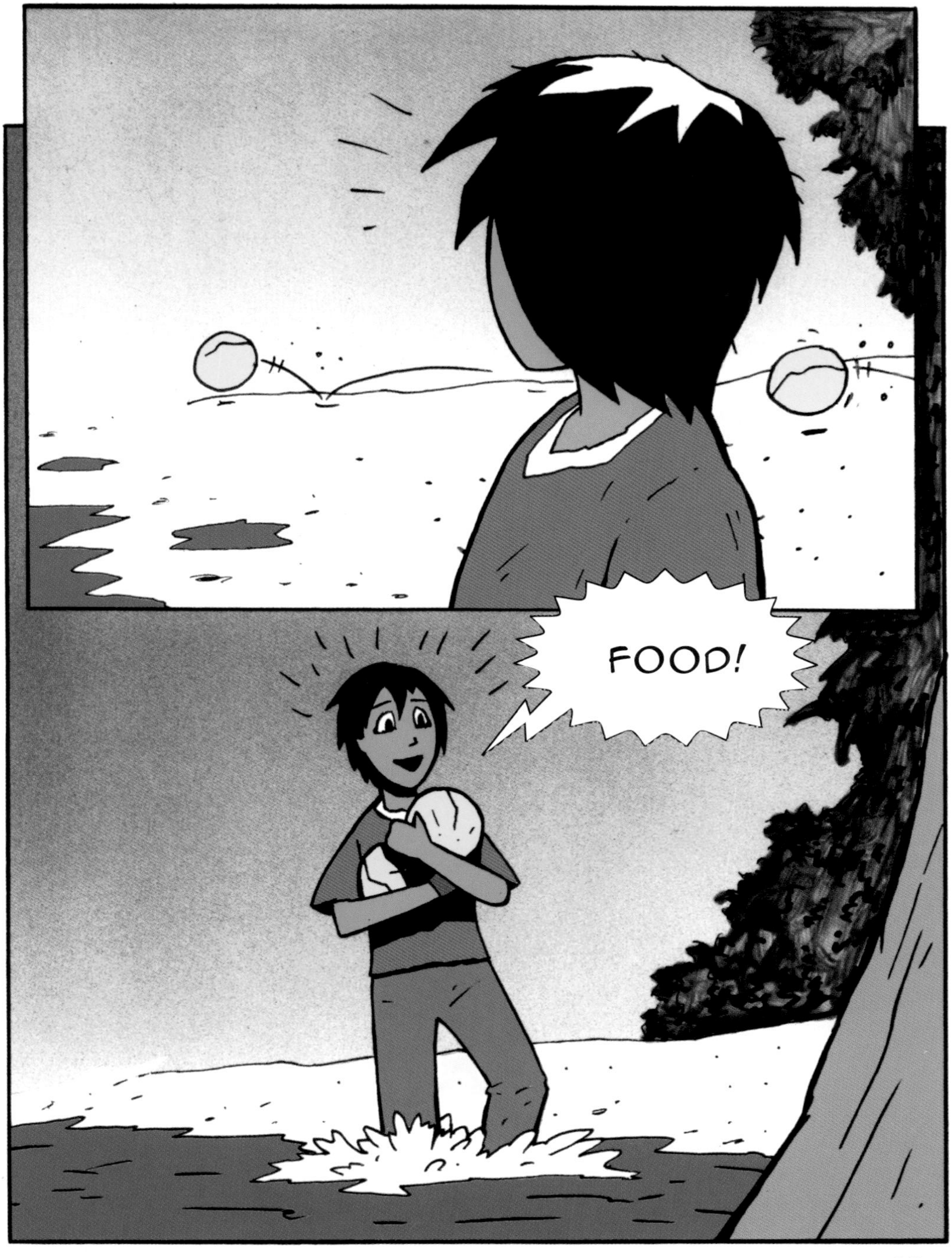
FOOD!

The surging water is now up to Nalini's chest. She knows it is powerful enough to knock her over, so she clutches the coconuts as she wades toward the cave.

"Nalini, throw them!" Zed says from the safety of the ledge above her. Nalini stands back and aims carefully, tossing the first coconut to Zed. He catches it with one hand and sets it beside him. "Now, the next one," he calls.

Nalini throws the second one, but it hits the rock and falls into the water. As the coconut floats away, Nalini swims after it.

"No, Nalini, leave it!" Zed shouts. Nalini doesn't listen. She reaches for the coconut, but it only floats farther away.

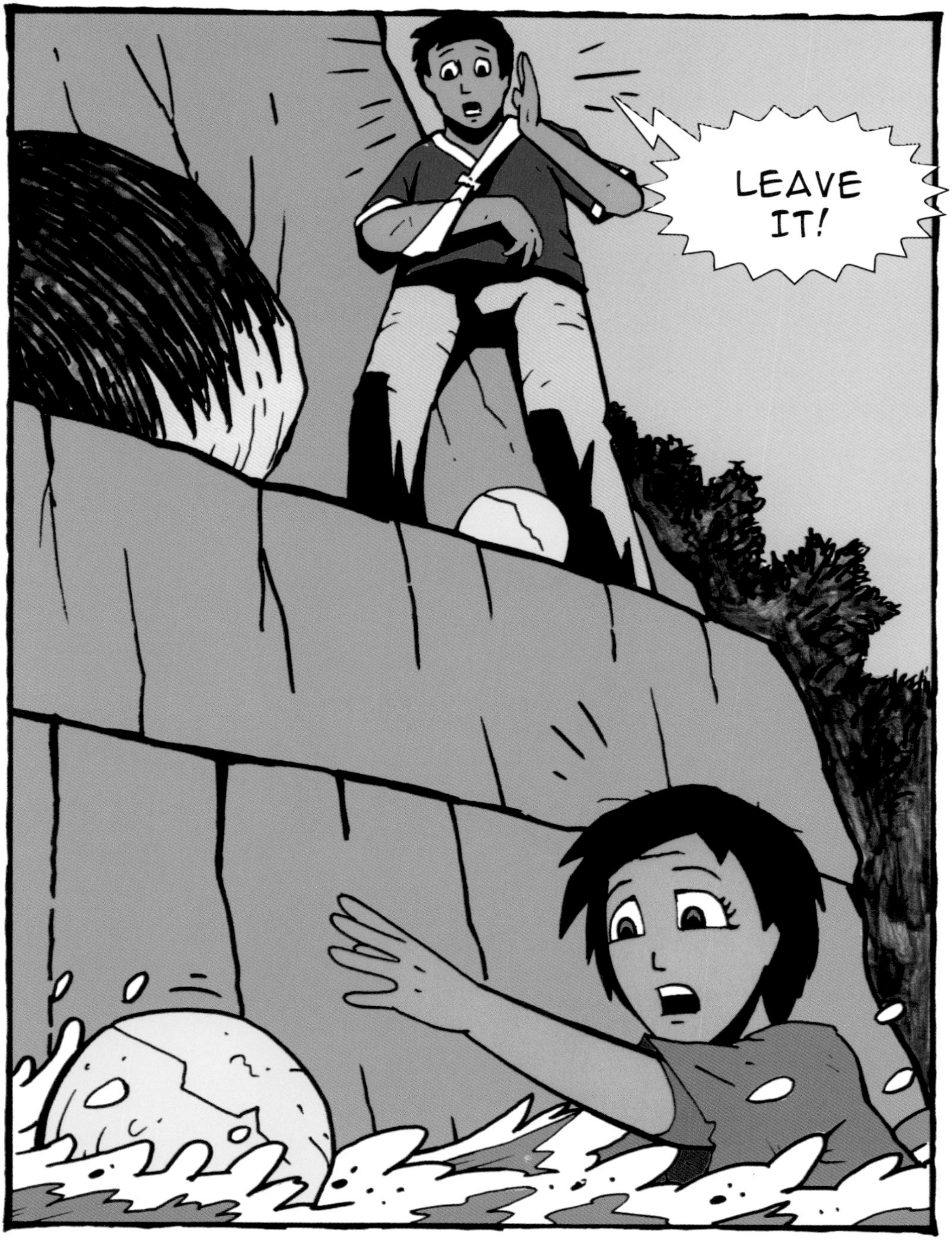
LEAVE IT!

A wave pushes Nalini against the rock wall. "One more try," she thinks, shoving away from the wall and lunging for the coconut. As she grabs the coconut, a wave pushes her under the water.

The wave moves over her, and her feet touch the bottom. When she stands up, the water is up to her neck.

"Nalini, quick!" Zed has moved halfway down the rocks, his foot extended to reach Nalini. She grabs his leg, and as the wave recedes, she is able to step onto the rocks. Zed and Nalini climb to the ledge, where they sit quietly for several minutes.

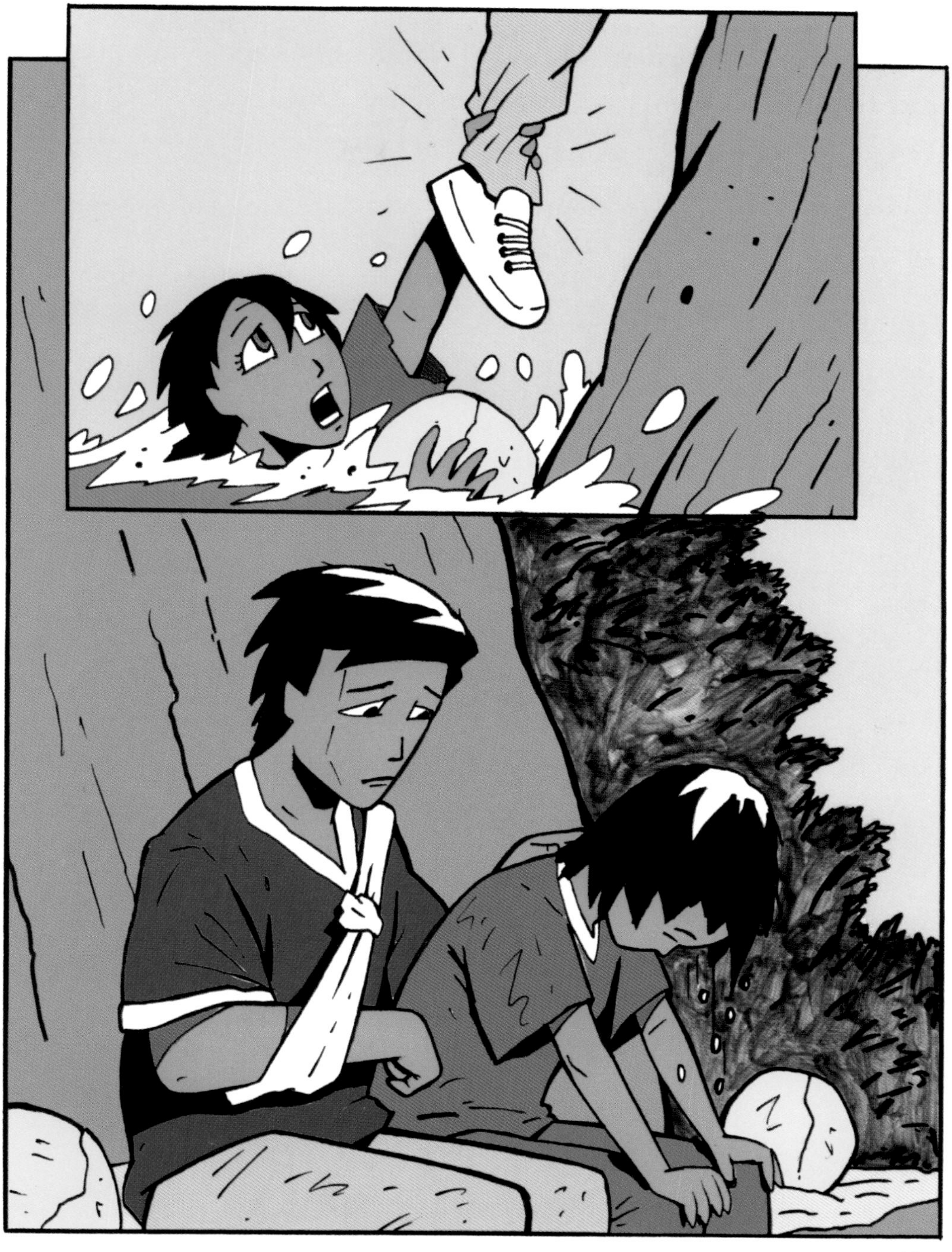

Using the crack down the side, Nalini opens a coconut. She breaks off a piece of white coconut meat, and they both eat some. It tastes sweet.

"How did you crack the coconuts, Nalini?" Zed asks.

"I didn't crack them—they had cracks when I found them," Nalini says.

"What about the empty coconuts for the water? How did you put the holes in them?" Zed asks.

"I didn't put holes in them," Nalini replies.

Zed is silent. "Who is cracking the coconuts and putting holes in them?" he thinks.

Nalini remembers the coconuts she found rolling down the beach. She also remembers the ashes that indicated someone had lit a fire in the cave.

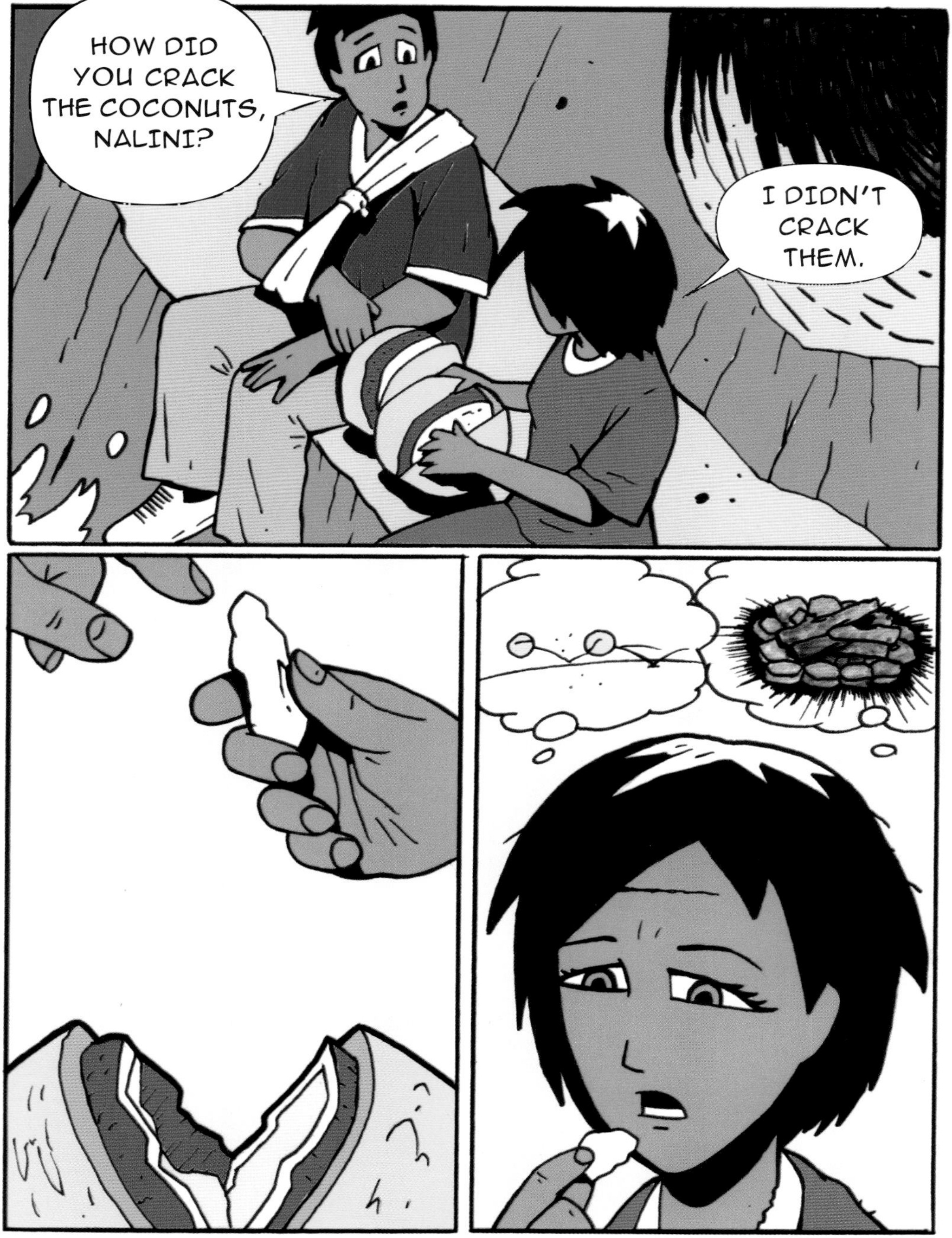
HOW DID YOU CRACK THE COCONUTS, NALINI?
I DIDN'T CRACK THEM.

"Zed, maybe we're not alone," she says.

Zed leans against the rock wall and nods. "Maybe," he says.

Nalini moves closer to her brother and asks, "Zed, will someone find us?"

"They are looking for us already," Zed replies, glancing at the sky.

Nalini leans back and gazes at the sea. "Tomorrow I want to catch a fish," she says.

"And I want to make a fire," Zed says.

As they watch the sunset, Nalini says, "We'll be all right, Zed."

"Yes," Zed responds, "we can take care of each other."

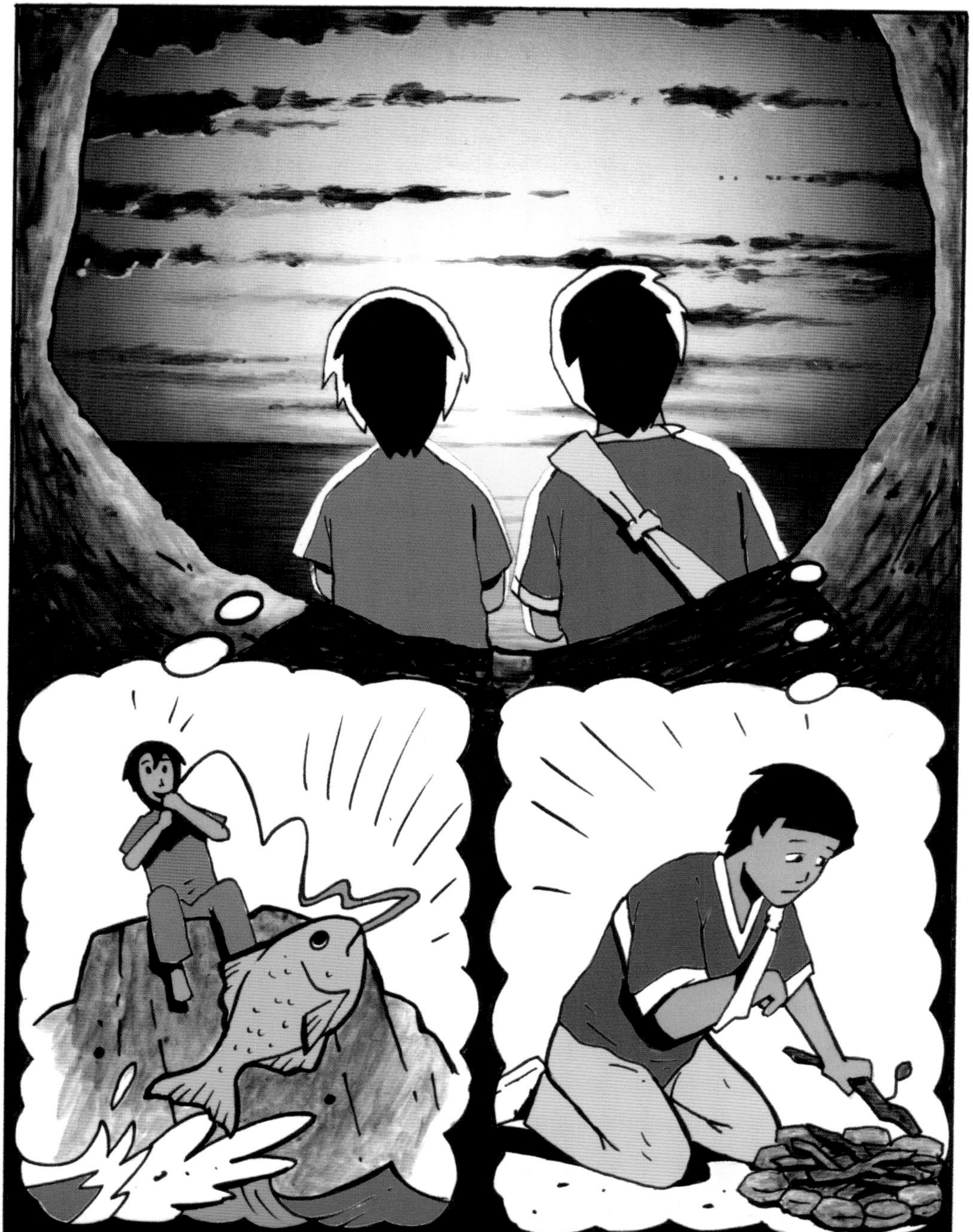

Glossary

debris (*noun*) the parts left when something is broken or destroyed

drenched (*adjective*) completely wet

illuminates (*verb*) lights up; brings attention to

irritably (*adverb*) in an angry and short way, as if irritated

lunging (*adjective*) moving forward suddenly

recedes (*verb*) moves back or away

rummaging (*adjective*) searching quickly

surge (*noun*) a swelling or growing movement like that of a wave

survived (*verb*) stayed alive

threatening (*adjective*) dangerous or causing worry